OVIS
NORTH AMERICAN WILD SHEEP

by
GUY TILLETT

Photographs by
SERLE CHAPMAN

With a foreword from
DENNIS CAMPBELL
Executive Director – The Grand Slam Club

They appear like centurions of the crags, their heads encased in coiled horns of armor over robes of dusk or tan. From October and deep into the moons of frost, the canyons resound with their battles, the rams clashing heads for the right to the ewes. Dignified then and always, they strut and stand imposing, the spread of their barrel magnificent yet carried with grace on a dancer's tip-toes . . .

From The Trail Of Many Spirits *by Serle Chapman.*

. . . for Kathryn

ABOUT THE AUTHOR . . .

Guy Tillett has a bachelor's degree in biological science from Butler University in Indianapolis, Indiana and a master's degree in biology from Indiana University in Bloomington. He taught Natural Science in secondary schools in Indiana for 10 years and has served as an educator and college administrator at National College in Rapid City, South Dakota for about 30 years. Tillett is an avid outdoorsman and spends considerable time in the field hunting, fishing, photographing, guiding, searching for arrowheads and enjoying the western environment and wildlife. He is a member of a number of organizations including the National Wildlife Federation, the Rocky Mountain Elk Foundation, the National Parks and Conservation Association, the National Wild Turkey Foundation, Trout Unlimited, the Foundation for North American Wild Sheep, the Pope and Young Club, the Natural Resources Defense Council, and others.

. . . AND PHOTOGRAPHER

Author and photographer Serle Chapman's first book, *The Trail Of Many Spirits*, was published in the UK on October 24, 1996. The first printing of the book sold out in under twelve weeks. His writing background stems from freelance journalism and magazine editing. In 1994 he won two national design and marketing awards for Further Education publications. His photography is on permanent display at the Las Vegas Natural History Museum, the National Bighorn Sheep Interpretive Center and in exhibitions across the USA. His work for the InterTribal Bison Cooperative has appeared in Audubon Magazine, and the World Society For The Protection of Animals use his photography. One of Europe's leading photography magazines, *Amateur Photographer*, included *The Trail Of Many Spirits* within its 1996 'Books of the Year'. Serle Chapman is supported by **American Airlines®**.

ACKNOWLEDGEMENTS

There have been several indirect and direct sources of support for this project. The videocassettes of the late Gordon Eastman, Duncan Gilchrist, Michael Dee Rogers and John Lewton provided detail and perspective on Bighorns. Dennis Campbell of the Grand Slam Club in Alabama offered valuable explanations. Glen Hisey of Pope and Young, and Jack Reneau of Boone and Crockett, also provided assistance and important input. Ramona L. Finley and the staff of the National Bighorn Sheep Interpretive Center in Dubois, Wyoming contributed greatly. Gina Penn Schneider of the Buffalo Bill Historic Center in Cody, Wyoming offered information regarding the Chadwick ram. The Foundation for North American Wild Sheep, also in Cody, provided valuable perspectives. Ted Benzon and Bruce Bessken, offered insight and assistance with Badlands bighorns. Gary Brundige provided valuable explanations. The Arizona Sonora Desert Museum, Tucson, were accommodating. Michael Francis and Mike Wolforth shared select images. Special thanks to Bear Print, Roundhouse Publishing and Mountain Press, and the creative and technical contributions of their associates who made the production of *Ovis* possible: Ken Bond, Sarah Gilbertson, Peter Casey, John Parker, Paul Wilson and Eric Tomlinson. Sketch of Guy Tillett by Howard R. Hanson.

Cover photo: Rocky Mountain Bighorn Ram, Black Hills, South Dakota.
Back cover photo: Ute Rock Art, Arches National Park, Utah.
All photographs are by Serle Chapman unless credited below:
© Michael H. Francis – page 38 *(Dall and Stone)*. © Mike Wolforth – pages 35 *(Badlands Bighorns)* and 36.
© Guy Tillett – pages 12, 13, 20, 21, 42 *(Bottom left)*, 43 *(Ghost and bottom right)*, 56 and 73.

Book design and layout: Serle Chapman. Digital Artwork: Ken Bond. Produced by: Bear Print. Photographic hand prints (color): Peter Casey. Digital reproduction: Colour Concept, Seacroft, Leeds, UK. Printed in the UK by Joseph Ward Colourprint. Proofread by Ken Blower.

First Edition.
ISBN: 0-9528607-2-4
Library Of Congress Catalog Card Number: 97-73565

Available from:
MOUNTAIN PRESS PUBLISHING COMPANY

PO Box 7581 Rapid City SD 57709-7581 USA
Bear Print: PO Box 244 Cambridge CB5 8YL UK

1301 So. Third Street West Missoula
MT 59806 Toll Free 1-800-234-5308

Roundhouse Publishing Group Limited
PO Box 140 Oxford OX2 7FF United Kingdom

CONTENTS

PREFACE   6

FOREWORD   7

INTRODUCTION   9

NATURAL HISTORY   11

LORE   23

MANAGEMENT   29

HUNTING   37

TAXONOMY   53

BIGHORNS & THINHORNS   57

DESERT BIGHORNS   59

ROCKY MOUNTAIN BIGHORNS   63

DALL'S SHEEP   67

STONE'S SHEEP   71

ENDNOTES   74

BIBLIOGRAPHY   74

PREFACE
by Guy Tillett

ith an existence of three score plus years, one begins to consider the significance and contemporaneous nature of life. Memory, the senses, energy, muscle and joint function and other qualities do not seem to exist at levels which previously existed, and were taken for granted. It is hoped that in this project, the words, figures, photographs and drawings will provide information and understanding, even inspiration for a particular audience. Also an inventory of quality experiences comes to the forefront, and small numbers of friends and family predominate, including seasonal interactions with wildlife and nature intertwined.

Spring returns with a wild flower sequence of pasque, shooting stars, and bluebells. The wild turkey rituals of gobbling and strutting are prominent. In summer, pods of rising rainbow and brown trout snatch nymphs and spinners of mayflies from the surface of rapidly moving cold water. There are occasional calls of the western tanager in the tall pines, and the ever present song of the meadowlark on the prairie comes to mind. In the fall, the frantic activity of the pronghorn in his rutting season, and the scream and bugle of the bull elk in the higher hills stands out. The flocks of sandhill cranes greet us from high above as they fly toward Nebraska. In winter and the last month of the year, I have been indebted to the bighorn sheep on French Creek for letting me observe them so closely, and I marvel at the energy, endurance, and the force of impact of rival rams as they physically test each other. The sound of the smashing horns continues to echo from the rock walls in the canyon, and that is how it should be. Snow, cold, and increased darkness settle over the land and the circle of life is small, but complete.

FOREWORD
by Dennis Campbell

Guy Tillett definitely covers a lot of ground in this work on North American wild sheep. His style tends toward a biological point of view, but by the time you finish you should realize that he has pretty much covered the spectrum.

Even though I had seen Guy's name tossed around a little in conservation circles, I have not as yet met him face to face. My first direct contact came when he called with a *few* questions about the Grand Slam Club. As is my way with something I am so passionate about, I went into more detail than I probably should have. After that initial conversation, I have since spoken with Guy on several occasions. One of those occasions was when he asked me to do this Foreword. I could not resist the opportunity to be a small part of a book about wild sheep.

I have been involved with wild sheep for close to 20 years now. I have been writing about these beloved animals for almost that long. My involvement with the Grand Slam Club stretches back almost 15 years, with half of that being as Executive Director. With this perspective, one thing I know . . . sheep enthusiasts and hunters just seemingly never get enough to read! When Guy Tillett called, doing research for this book, I knew he was onto a winner.

I personally appreciate the work Guy has put into *OVIS*. He has captured the 'big picture' as concerns wild sheep. Read on, and *you* will come away with a better understanding of the many aspects of our precious North American wild sheep.

Rocky Mountain bighorns

INTRODUCTION

It may be that North American wild sheep are the most revered of all wild ungulate mammals on the continent. The passion for wild sheep felt by artists, scientists, photographers, observers, hunters, and others is extreme and rivaled by empathy for only a few other species. white-tail deer are so familiar and wide-spread and the majestic elk through sheer physical proportions certainly have their followings.

The aura of North American wild sheep and its impact on our kind is pervasive and indiscriminate. It is historically, mystically, and scientifically based with other less distinct emergent qualities. Trying to verbalize feelings for these life forms may be as impossible as trying to qualify a taste for chocolate, describing a fragrance of lilacs, or explaining a basis for one's favorite color. Wild sheep are rare, yet far from endangered; they are exotic if for nothing other than their remote natural habitats, and certainly they are among the most beautiful of wild animals. Perhaps a relative scarcity relates to the esteem. The invigoration produced by experiencing the mountain vistas or the sense of isolation and humility derived from a quest for an encounter with sheep flavors the sensibilities.

That those who choose to hunt sheep or other animals may experience deep, personal feelings for wildlife seems to present a contradiction for some who wish not to hunt or those who are distressed by elements of the practice. Please recognize that for most the feelings are there, and for many that hunt there may be a degree of admiration or veneration that cannot be experienced in any other way. May we set this quandry aside and extol *Ovis canadensis* – the Bighorns, *Ovis dalli* – the Thinhorns, and their well known subspecies.

Rocky Mountain bighorn ram

NATURAL HISTORY

If one considers evolutionary principles, Charles Darwin's contributions would be particularly significant. Genetics would require the inclusion of Gregor Mendel's activity and taxonomy would credit Karl Von Linne (*Linnaeus*). Similarly, any approach to the natural history of North American wildlife species would call for the notations of Ernest Thompson Seton, the naturalist, artist, and author of the seven volume set, *Lives of Game Animals* (1929). Seton's treatise is on 'land animals in America north of the Mexican border, which are considered game because they have held the attention of sportsmen, or have received the protection of law'. These works are a product of earlier times, but present exhaustive detail and quips, and any who are fortunate enough to own them or have access will find the information therein entertaining and educational. Volume Three, Part II includes sections on the 'The Bighorn' and 'The White Sheep'. The behavior of wild sheep today is not unlike the behavior and curiosities in Seton's time.

To carry this sequence one step further, it seems appropriate to acknowledge Valerius Geist as at least one prominent authority on wild sheep. He is an accomplished writer and one who concerns himself with issues related to wild sheep, their behavior and their place in the natural environment. Professor Geist is a program director of environmental sciences at the

University of Calgary, Alberta, Canada. Conservation, management, and ethology are focal areas for Dr Geist.

Sheep yes, but like the domestic forms in physical and behavioral terms, not at all. There are many physical differences including the hair, and that of wild sheep is more like that of the deer family and not wool-like. The coat color varies with the species and with the season, but it is of short, smooth hair. The meat of the wild sheep does not have the taste of mutton. It is not like that of the domestics and its quality may diminish only slightly during the rut or with age.

Ovis, the genus for North American wild sheep is also a designation for some old-world and ancient forms, of perhaps two and one half million years ago. North American wild sheep are believed to have originated in Eurasia; and some of these came to North America by way of the Bering Strait.[1] This possibly took place in the same way, and perhaps around the same time, as that of the human migrations onto this continent. In the same way that Native American populations: Eskimo, Hawaiian, American Indians, etc, had little or no immunity to the diseases brought to them by the European traders, missionaries, soldiers, pioneers, etc; the North American wild sheep are sensitive to the parasites and ailments found in domestic stock that accompanied the same individuals. North American wild sheep, probably from Siberian stock, are not particularly well equipped to deal with illnesses or predators outside the harsh Eurasian cold and dry climate and environments. The speciation of *Ovis* is likely a

"Front kick"

12

product of group isolation, perhaps initiated or accelerated during the glacial periods.

Wild forms are much quieter than the more 'talkative' domestics (*Ovis aries*). The calls between the wild ewes and lambs range from urgent to simple reassurance in the forms of soft 'bleats' and 'blatts'. Wild rams occasionally vocalize by a grunt or snort. When upset they seem to grind their teeth to dramatize their mood.

One of the interesting aspects of wild sheep behavior is that related to the body language of the rams, and the intricacies of those expressions. These are most evident at the time of the rut (breeding) and many relate to assertions of dominance over lesser rams or the ewes. Males gather in groups of roughly comparable size and age and on occasion stand almost body to body, resembling the 'huddle' of athletic teams. It is at these times that 'who can lick whom' priorities are begun or reinforced. 'Horning', a tribute which is paid to the senior members, occurs at this time and other times as well. The horns are rubbed against the body and face of more dominant rams, and the motivation for this in part may be to pick up glandular scents. 'Front kicks' or striking out with the front leg, the 'low stretch', a cocking or 'twisting' of the head and horns, a 'chin up' posture which presents the horn mass prominently, are factors involved in variable sequences intended to help establish dominance standings. The 'low stretch' and several other of these postures were described by Valerius Geist in his detailed studies and writings regarding wild sheep.[2] The 'low stretch' is descriptive of a low slung head-down approach that is somewhat

"Low stretch"

13

like that of the rutting buck deer. Dominant rams employ these and even courtship behaviors to emphasize their superiority over lesser males.

The environmental homes of wild sheep are remote, in some ways bleak and dangerous, yet spectacular and inspiring. Bighorns are born on the edge of the world . . . at least their world. The birthplace is often a ledge, usually near a steep slope, and the arrival is timed for early summer or spring, depending upon the latitude. The ewe, like many other mammalian mothers, consumes birth fluids and membranes to return required elements to her physical makeup and reduce the signals that might prompt predation.

The terrain utilized by wild sheep is particularly significant and must offer security for lambing, limited contact with competitive species, and means to avoid predation. Rugged landscapes that offer slopes for sunning, shelter from winds, and precipitous passage is the preferred topography.

Birth is timed to associate with the growth and development of grasses, flowers and other foliage, because the lambs start on solid food only a few days after being born. Gestation is approximately six months (typically 175 days) which is relatively short compared to that of other ungulates (elk, musk ox, caribou, etc). Twins are infrequent for mountain sheep, which is understandable considering the harsh environment and limited food available for pregnant females during gestation. Also, if twins were the rule rather than the exception, each offspring would necessarily be smaller in body mass, and as such vulnerable to the cold (according to Bergman's Rule)

and less likely to gain the weight to allow them to deal with a short summer and a long and severe winter. These northern lambs must attain an optimal size at birth to achieve survival.

The lambs are precocious but dependent upon their mothers for nutrition and protection. The ewes' horns are only a fraction of those of the rams but they are sharp and the mother's efforts are valiant when she and her offspring are challenged. Golden eagles are a menace but only very few are successful in killing a young lamb. Eagles are known to feed on the carcasses of fallen sheep, either wild or domestic, young or old. Other natural enemies include lynx, mountain lions, bobcats, wolves, coyotes, wolverines, bears, etc. Man might also be listed as a mortal enemy of sheep, but regulated hunting and the efforts of several organized groups in acquiring and augmenting habitat has actually improved wild sheep welfare and range. In this context the Foundation for North American Wild Sheep (FNAWS, Cody, Wyoming), and several other state and private groups committed to wildlife management have brightened the future for wild sheep. Overall loss of habitat, poaching, and encroachment by feral animals (particularly burros), man's domestic sheep and other domestics continues to add to the complexity of the relationship between man and wild sheep. Contact with livestock, particularly domestic sheep is very hazardous for wild sheep.

Growth of the lambs is rapid and after a few days they join a nursery group and in this 'day care' setting they play games, frolic, butt heads and generally wear out the less rambunctious ewes that are in some way designated to guard the flock. Sentinels are important here and in almost all other wild sheep gatherings. Nursery groups are managed by older ewes and at times other than play, rather strict discipline is maintained. Young rams remain with the ewes until their third year.

Like others in this biological group of ruminants, food is chewed, swallowed, and brought up from the rumen, the first of four divisions of the stomach for a more leisurely repast. Sheep are very selective and strict vegetarians, favoring certain grasses when available. The Desert bighorns are opportunistic grazers but are more inclined to browse on fruit, flowers, leaves and stems of native plants including cacti. Sheep diets are supplemented by minerals from salt licks. They eat certain kinds of crumbling rock or soil and even sample roadside minerals.

Included in the special interest areas of mountain sheep are their sure-footedness, stamina, and nonchalance in racing up, down, and over steep terrain. Occasional falls, snow slides, and rock slides are a cause of death for the wild sheep. Snow and ice associated with cold temperatures present problems because they cover needed food sources. At times this can be so severe as to require some migration and at these times extensive movement adds to the danger and hazard. Sheep and mountain goats on occasion seek the shelter of caves or overhangs, and they may even share the same space during extended storms.[3] In the caves or sheltered spots the droppings are often several inches thick, and have accumulated for years.

Migration for Desert bighorns relates to finding suitable water for drinking. Water is the most serious physiological problem for these sheep. With a shortage, dominance and peck order priorities prevail and the lambs and younger sheep suffer. Desert bighorns perspire to help regulate body heat, and dog-like panting is also employed to help dissipation.

Not many wild sheep succumb to old age; they are more likely to fall victim to forms of violence. Even highways and trains pose serious threats to bands of sheep. Old age is from 10 to 14 years but there are exceptional instances of 20-year-old rams.

The disease scabies has been strongly contributive to sheep mortality. Whether the wild form gave this to the domestics, or the other way around, depends upon whom you ask. A form of pneumonia may present the biggest threat to wild sheep. This disorder is usually secondary and is triggered by lungworm infections, viral disorders or a bacterial (*Pasturella sp.*) infection. High density populations or proximity to domestic sheep tends to result in physical stress related to depleted forage which often produces minor or major die offs. Other internal and external parasites similarly combine with unfavorable conditions to trigger pneumonia or hemorrhagic septicemia and fatalities.[4] Wild sheep evidence unusual susceptibility to pneumonia and other lung diseases. Ticks are common and the ears of some of the older animals my become plugged or infected by irritation from ticks.

Lungworms in otherwise healthy sheep are overcome by encapsulation in scar tissue which diminishes lung elasticity and effectively reduces respiratory capacity. Older rams and ewes are tested during the intensity of the rut when physical exertion is the norm. These animals seem to accept their limitations and do less running but often accomplish more than an ample share of breeding through calculated and deliberate acts instead of the wild and frantic exertion and fervor associated with youth. The rut is physically demanding, exhausting and a major drain on health and physical capabilities, especially with breeding males. There are also often very serious injuries sustained.

Not all disorders of wild sheep are so grim in their outcome. Contagious ecthyma is a dermatitis that occurs around the mouths of lambs and non-immune adults, most often during the early spring. It is a viral disease that may lie dormant in a sheep range and produce an outbreak after an absence of several years, even 10 or 12. The oral lesions are prominent and appear similar to cold sores, complete with bleeding, swelling, and ulceration. The course of the disease is run in one to four weeks and the affected tissue heals and some measure of immunity from future infection is gained. The tenderness of the mouth may discourage normal eating and weaken particular animals toward a secondary infection. A more serious viral disease called bluetongue that adversely affects cattle, domestic sheep and deer, may also occasionally be transmitted to wild sheep.

The eyesight of wild sheep is incredibly good and the senses of smell and hearing are also acute but not

Bighorn lamb

so extreme. The prominent amber eyes are jewel-like and the acuity is among the best of all mammals. References to the eyesight of sheep and pronghorn antelope often compare their vision to the effects of 8x or 10x binoculars but this correlation remains a point of conjecture.

Weight and some other physical features vary with the species, variety, age, and sex, but adult rams may be expected to weigh 200 pounds and ewes up to 150. There are occasional 300 pound rams and in the case of bighorns, the individuals in northern ranges tend to be physically larger. The ratio of body volume or mass and surface area, which contributes to heat loss, is described as Bergman's Rule and it can be applied here as well as with several other closely related mammals and birds. This ratio correlates with increasing northern latitudes, so the Desert bighorns are and should be expected to be physically smaller than their northern relatives. Allen's Rule similarly relates the extremities of mammals and birds according to a southern latitude distribution. Merriam's wild turkey, the northernmost of the wild turkey subspecies, has the shortest legs. Predictably the bighorns in Alberta or Dall's rams will have ears and faces smaller than those of the Desert bighorn living on the United States and Mexican border. What is happening, as described by both rules, is conservation of heat energy and body temperature control according to surroundings. Bergman's Rule reverses for wild sheep and perhaps some other North American species at extreme northern latitudes. In other words the body of Dall's sheep is typically

Desert bighorn panting

smaller than that of Stone's sheep, which are found farther south. Physical conditions are affected by the elevation of habitat which corresponds to higher latitudes. Coloration in a number of temperate and northern birds and mammals also follows the pattern, with a presence of white increasing in the north.

The massive horns of the rams present a most interesting feature and they generate much interest among those who seek the animals as wildlife trophies. Horn size, like antler mass, is a function of genetics, age, sex, and nutrition. Horns, which may weigh up to 40 pounds on mature males, are a secondary sex characteristic that adorn the male and add to his virility in the view of others of his species, particularly the females. In evolutionary terms the implication of this is that a particular male is desirable from the standpoint of being physically well, and well-to-do in a biological sense. He has the genes, he has the health, and he has occupied the range to permit him to divert energy and nutrition into this mass of material upon his head. The head-gear then demonstrates his status among those of his kind and the more the better, at least to a point. Many males may persist in the rut to gain sexual favors, but the females will make the determinations in accordance with perpetual 'survival of the fittest' incentives. The ewe is active in discouraging male pursuers. She selects difficult terrain and arranges her body so that breeding is difficult or awkward. She also walks away at opportune times frustrating the younger and less desirable suitors.

The largest head of a wild North American ram ever taken was that of the Chadwick Ram, a British Columbian Stone's sheep. Its horns measured (green score) 52⅛ inches on the curvature, with 15 plus inches on the bases and a tip to tip spread of 31¼ inches. The mounted head is described as the finest trophy specimen of all game animals ever taken, a considerable distinction. It was described initially as being 14 years old, and it is housed at the Firearms Museum at the Buffalo Bill Historic Center in Cody, Wyoming.

Rams can be aged on the ground and to some extent on the hoof, on the basis of counting the number of more rugged cross-ridge rings on the horn with each being the equivalent of one year. The ends of the horns, the lamb tips, are often missing and 'broomed' by the wearer to permit less obstructed vision. The fourth year on many rams is the most prominent of these ridges between wrinkles and by counting from number four back toward the head one can assess age. The fourth year ridge is more distinctive from the back of the horn. Each major ring or ridge indicates a cessation of growth for the year, not unlike tree rings which are similarly used. There are also seasonal rings which are less distinct and are interspersed between annual rings. The annual rings are not evenly distributed and they become less distinct nearer the head, particularly on older rams.

The horns of wild sheep are permanent and continue to grow throughout the life of the animal. They are composed of a material called keratin, which is also present in the hooves, and in the external tissues of several other vertebrate animals.

The rams themselves seem to direct much attention to the horns of other rams, seeking company of familiar and comparable individuals. The male behaviors and rituals often relate to horn mass, with displays and assertions of the same to maximum advantage. These ritualized displays may intimidate other males and assist in the seduction of females. The rams are promiscuous and their attention to the ewes relates exclusively to their estrous cycle and approaching receptivity. By remaining in proximity and fighting for 'pole position' when required, the lucky ram participates in procreation. At these times the 'lip curls' (flehmen) to test the females and the intimidation and jousting of other males describe common behaviors of the rams. The sexual prowess of the ram is perhaps enviable in that he can mate with several ewes in just a few minutes. He is not like the elk or pronghorn which collect harems. The ram is simply excited by and consumed by his hormones and the mating behavior.

Sometimes horn displays or gestures are not enough and during the mating season mountain sheep rams dispense with gestures and enter into a well-choreographed and sometimes brutal sequence. In this combat the inferior individual usually initiates the confrontation and various postures, stares and insults inflame combat. The gauntlet may include the front leg strikes and vocalizations. An uphill advantage adds a bit of gravitational force to the challenger's impact. The standoff space is established and powerful hind quarters pile drive the horns, skull and massive neck and shoulders into the equivalent parts of the suitably matched opponent. In many instances both rams raise their bodies and charge on rear legs and at the last second they drop toward each other adding the energy of the fall into the blow.

The larger ram attempts to accept the blow in the area between its own horns, but both suffer the energy of impact. Usually the chins are raised quickly in braggadocio and to emphasize the impressive qualities of their horns. At this point the larger ram may take higher ground or at least the initiative and he becomes the aggressor 'pitching his best stuff' to the upstart receiver. The force of these sledge-hammer blows sounds like a strike in a bowling alley, and on a calm day the 'crack' can be heard for a mile or even two. Once or twice is rarely enough, so time after time the jealous rivals square off and charge. A massive rounded bulge of fibrous tissue, the nuchal tendon behind the horns and near the base of the skull receives much of the impact energy. This knobby mass of tissue becomes more prominent and plausibly more functional in absorption of blows to the horns, head, neck, and cervical portions of the spine. The skull of the rutting ram is also much heavier and thicker than that of the ewes or younger rams.

Horns split, pieces are lost, and sometimes blood flows from the ears and nose as occurs in a concussion. With each impact the warriors appear somewhat dazed. Members of the flock, including other rams gather to observe the battle and occasionally some of them join the fray. These confrontations may go on for several hours but one or the other of the combatants ultimately falters. Squinting or breaking visual contact (a 'blink' in the display ritual) is a signal that the towel is about to be thrown in. To stumble or fall, or being knocked off all fours identifies the winner and loser. The loser can surrender or strike a truce by simply turning away and grazing. When these standings are established an insult of courtship gestures and even mounting helps affirm dominance, which is what the fight was all about anyway. The other option available to the loser is to leave the band and the immediate area. To stay means to submit to bullying and other derogatory acts. Champions are rewarded with breeding rights, but these high honors are short-lived because there is always an emerging bachelor seeking love and war.

Other than during the rut, matched rams gather amiably and often assemble in mutual-admiration-society groups. These ram 'huddles' usually precede the rut and they may relate to the physical and mental preparations. The 'peck-order' standings are established through these gatherings, previous encounters or the various displays of horns, the postures and other acts of dominance. Mountain sheep are particularly gregarious, although the sexes remain apart except for the rut. Wild sheep are only rarely solitary. Flocks or bands may range from a dozen to two or three dozen in a group.

Sheep in some settings become particularly tolerant of humans when science, photography or other less violent motives or objectives are being served. These sheep learn that a human presence presents no

". . . seeking love . . ."

particular threat. This is described as habituation. In this context one should not stare at or stalk the sheep, and they should be permitted some reasonable separation distance which can usually be determined on the basis of their response. If the sheep move away you are probably too close. Approach the sheep indirectly and conspicuously. Wild sheep can become so tolerant as to proceed in investigating humans. Curious and usually shy sheep can become pesky or even entertaining when this occurs, but it is probably not in the best interest of the sheep. This tendency probably relates to domestication of sheep early in man's history. Sheep were probably among the earliest of human beings' successful domestications. If the wild sheep, particularly the rams, take an initiative or seem to be asserting dominance by a 'low stretch', a 'twist' of the head, or other gestures, it is most likely not in the observers best interest and the contact should be broken. A human is going to be the loser in a head butting, dominance challenge with a wild ram. It is very important to be aware of any signals that are being sent by the animal's body language. Harassment of wildlife must be avoided.

Wild sheep will often use the same bedding spot repeatedly or they may use the bed of another sheep. They usually scratch out the area before lying down. When completely at rest, the chin is often placed on the ground and rams will lean their head and rest a horn on the ground so that weight can be supported during sleep. At rest or during sleep, a ram will also quite often extend a foreleg. Like pronghorn, wild sheep seem to move about very little during the hours of darkness.

". . . and war ."

Ute rock art

LORE

Stone-age hunters in parts of North America pecked the images (petroglyphs) into the patina (desert varnish) on vertical rock faces. Perhaps these Neolithic artists/hunters were commemorating a game animal acquisition or perhaps it was a totem for an event yet to occur. Whether the wild sheep were abundant or just popular is not clear. Sheep are among the most prevalent of animal figures (zoomorphs) in prehistoric art for most of the western area. Perhaps this commemorative activity is not so different from the wildlife art and the mounted heads that grace the walls of modern trophy hunters. Mountain sheep usually occupy special places in today's trophy rooms.

The 'Old Ones' that preceded recognizable Native American groups who occupied a region which includes the Colorado Plateau, were dependent upon mountain sheep. Many were as reliant on the sheep as the Plains Indians were upon the bison. Mountain sheep were the direct source of food and clothing, while horns and bones provided a source for various tools and utensils. Some archeological sites in the Southwest reveal that wild sheep were a favored food source as indicated by a predominance of their bones, compared to those of other game animals. The ram's horn could be reduced to spoons and ladles. Embers could be carried and soups could be served in a bighorn sheep's horn. Reconstructing life styles requires some speculation, but primitive rock art presents prehistory and the prominence of and dependence upon wild sheep by the 'Old Ones'.

In Nine Mile Canyon of the Uinta Basin in Northeastern Utah, the 'Great Hunting Scene' depicts 43 figures, of which 33 are mountain sheep. Likenesses of hunters surrounding wild sheep are pecked into the rock face. One hunter may be acting as a decoy wearing a sheep hide, while another human figure seems to have tethered a wild sheep. Over the centuries similar encounters have been rendered in rock art form, extending with the range of wild sheep over a thousand miles.

At another time in another place, a large Medicine Wheel was constructed in the Bighorn Mountains of Wyoming, not far from Sheep Mountain, between Sheridan and Lovell. The giant wheel, an enigma in our modern day, may have been a resource or a center of a culture that needed to regulate activities through something tangible. Perhaps there was a need to promulgate beliefs and spirituality in terms of the stars, the seasons and other mysteries of life. Twenty-eight spokes of arranged rock radiate from a large central stone cairn. Certain of these spokes end in smaller cairns (alters). A few years ago when visiting the site, a sheep skull had been honorably placed before one of the smaller cairns. It seemed that some individual, or perhaps a group of Shoshone or Crow people, may have recently placed the skull. It is reasonable to think that similar acts may have taken place when Native Americans assembled at the Medicine Wheel in centuries past. It may have been the predecessors of the Shoshone or Cheyenne who first frequented the Bighorns. An account by a Tukadüka, or Sheep Eater, elder, identifies the twenty-eight spokes as representing the individual bands that formed her people's nation.

Some early Native American groups described wild sheep in their oral history and traditions. The constellation Orion, the hunter, includes a prominence of three stars seen by some First American peoples as 'three Mountain sheep'. Those three stars are named (from the left) Alnitak, Alnilam, and Mintaka. What is presently described as the sword of the hunter, placed in the belt of the three stars, was previously a stone-tipped arrow shot into the middle sheep in the band of three.[5] The more familiar stars in the constellation which are of greater magnitude are Betelgeuse, Belatrix, Rigel, and Saiph.

Mountain tribes hung sheep horns in trees or piled up masses of sheep horns, perhaps to create a monument or a marker of some significance.[6] When wild sheep were killed by some early hunters, they were often butchered outside the village or the camp. To bring the carcass into the gathering might be to create unrest with the spirit of sheep. Bad things might occur, and the sheep might not be so accommodating in the future.[7] The Shoshone were strongly associated with mountain sheep. When Shoshone hunters brought down a sheep, the remains were respectfully situated away from camp with the head facing east. The morning star and other heavenly bodies, upon rising, could greet the fallen sheep, and contribute to the regeneration of its spirit.

Archeological research provides evidence for mountain sheep trapping by prehistoric Native American hunters. Evidently the sheep were driven along established lines which still exist to some extent in the form of stones, rock cairns, logs, and stumps and procurement was accomplished by funneling the flocks into traps, pits, or contrived catch pens.[8] Similar activity related to antelope, and in the case of bison the end of the line was a buffalo jump.

Some indigenous hunters prized bows made of antler (elk) or horn (bison, cattle, or mountain sheep), and of these the ones crafted from the outside curvature of the horn of the trophy bighorn ram was valued as physically and spiritually powerful, giving the owner much prestige. Rams of 30-40 inches of outside curve were used and great effort was required to boil and straighten portions of the horn, which also had to be clamped, dried, trimmed, and shaped and sanded before use. Often some degree of reflex curve was incorporated and much of this technology came after the arrival of the horse. Short and powerful bows were required to bring down large game such as bison and these huge animals were pursued on horseback. Bows of this nature were not numerous but were found in association with Shoshone, Nez Perce, Blackfoot, Kootenai, and Ute. Crow hunters also used the bow made from the horn of the ram and these were probably acquired in trade from the Shoshone.[9]

Teton Lakota bands carried the embers for ceremonial fires in the horn of a bighorn ram, and many Lakota men experienced visions which included the four-legged (elk, bighorns, wolves, etc). The 'sheep-dreamers' were organized into a warrior society, or cult, called 'They Dream Of Mountain Sheep', each member respected for being in possession of strong war medicine.

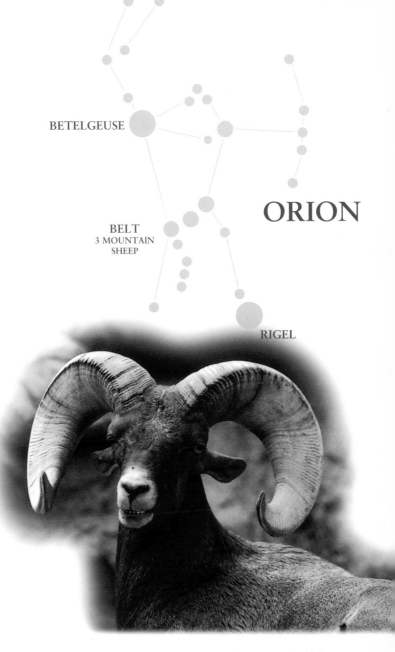

BETELGEUSE

ORION

BELT
3 MOUNTAIN
SHEEP

RIGEL

The Old One's buffalo . . .

25

Early white travelers and settlers assigned names to plants, animals and Native American groups that were less than scientific, and in the case of the Indians little regard was given to language, kinship, social order or cultural distinction. Shoshone and Paiutes were often referred to as 'Snakes'. In other instances groups were assembled on the basis of food commonly eaten, and the groundhog eaters, salmon eaters, and buffalo eaters emerged, if only briefly. The Tukadüka, 'The Sheep Eaters', were primarily Western Shoshoneans or Shoshokos, and Northern Bannocks. These were people who frequented what is now Yellowstone Park, and west into southern Montana and Idaho into the Sawtooth and Bitteroot ranges of the Rocky Mountains. These food-related distinctions were superficial and probably also related to Arapaho, Assiniboin and some others.[10]

Most Shoshones, including the Eastern and Comanche, identified themselves with a gesture that depicted the in-and-out motion of weaving, a throwback to previous generations who weaved their dwellings from grasses and bark. Other tribes misinterpreted the hand signal as serpentine and erroneously grouped them as 'Snakes', which some portion of the European interests picked up on. The Western Shoshone and Bannock made signs for 'eaters of sheep' to identify themselves. They used the sign for mountain sheep, not to be confused with the sign for domestic sheep that developed with the arrival of the Europeans and their livestock. One of the most revered Shoshone leaders, Togwotee or 'Spear It', was a Sheep Eater. Today, 'Togwotee Pass' runs close to the National Bighorn Sheep Interpretive Center, and on north of Dubois, Wyoming.

In the early 1800s Lewis and Clark described several Native American groups among whom eating sheep was common. They also recorded the presence of wild sheep along the mouth of the Judith River, Montana. Audubon's sheep, a race of bighorns, occupied the lowlands and several portions of the northern plains. The last known specimen was killed in Montana in 1916.[11] Other references indicated that the last Audubon's sheep (or Badlands bighorn) was killed at Magpie Creek, North Dakota in 1905. People in South Dakota would probably prefer that either North Dakota or Montana accept the responsibility.

The Pueblo-influenced cultures of the southwestern United States, which includes the Hopi and the Navajo, continue to use rams' horns in their headdresses on certain ceremonial occasions. The Apache and Navajo were known to have hunted mountain sheep before the Navajo acquired domestic sheep. These animals are important to the Navajo people in both economic and spiritual terms. The sheep are perceived to be a special gift and they were received with a spiritual admonition . . . 'Care for the sheep and you will always have life!'

Old-world historic and cultural associations with sheep would include the Celt's fascination with the spiral horns and their attributing of war-like qualities to rams. Islamic practices of sacrificing adult sheep and lambs for atonement is prominent in Biblical verse. Egyptians, *ca* 1320-1200 BC, identified a deity with the head of a ram and a human body. A striated headdress accentuated the horns.

Dall's   *Desert*   *Rocky Mountain*

Into the arms of Orion –
"Three Mountain Sheep"

Dall's sheep

MANAGEMENT

Wild rams may appeal more to the male intrigue. Men seem to relate to the aggression, dominance, social structure and rough-housing of rams and this bias carries over into naming sports teams, certain vehicles, and other forms of symbolism. Sport hunting and the sport hunting organizations which also promote sheep welfare are decidedly, but not exclusively, male dominated.

Single-minded support and advocacy of sheep could help contribute to their undoing. Single species wildlife organizations, including those that favor wild sheep, must consider broad ecological relationships, including the positives of predator and prey relationships, the impact of introducing non-native species into certain environments, water development practices and other environmental dynamics. The interdependence of a single species with others and with the natural environment is complex and often difficult to improve upon, even by well-meaning individuals and groups. The nature of the involvement, not the involvement *per se*, is the rub. This 'cats cradle' of interdependence requires that we pull strings only very carefully.

Original populations of wild North American sheep were isolated by environmental factors contributing to the creation of separate species and subspecies. Isolation has increased through political and economic practices further restricting these small

The family on the mountain – Rocky Mountain bighorns.

Rocky Mountain bighorn
ewe with lamb

populations. Sheep in small populations are vulnerable to environmental and biological pressures and may not survive. This is only in part resultant from inbreeding and the limitations of forage. In breeding and genetic terms small isolated populations are unhealthy.

Sheep tend not to extend their range or to go beyond the limits of predictable and established seasonal habitats. A lack of adaptability in wild sheep is a negative in man's efforts to manage them. These are creatures of habit and are in no way adventurous. They require an ecologically mature environment and they are intolerant of disturbance, conflict, or competition. The young sheep, male or female, do what their seniors do and thereby establish a behavior that becomes fixed, repetitive and cyclic until some natural or unnatural pressure alters that routine. Seasonal migrations are orderly and predictable, moving from square A to square B. Although squares C and D may seem to present the required elements in food and terrain, they are not part of the sequence and not programmed into the behavior of a particular group of sheep. These seasonal behavior routines are so precise as to occur at or near specific calendar dates. Sheep are then positioned at particular salt licks or breeding grounds according to the calendar, and with more continuity than should be expected.

When pressure occurs an area of comfort may be abandoned for less preferable terrain. Sheep may be driven into timber or they may be forced to seek other unfamiliar haunts, but only then with some sacrifice. Wild sheep longevity will require human involvement and finances beyond largely ineffective predator control and essentially productive water development projects. Transplant efforts and land acquisition are two of the measures to help maintain sheep populations.

White-tailed deer, particularly the young bucks, are active in seeking out new territories thereby helping to establish healthy breeding populations where they did not exist previously. This relocation also introduces alternate traits into the gene pool and helps insure vitality of that population. Wild sheep do not usually exhibit this tendency toward dispersal although it does occur on a limited basis when ranges and habitats occasionally change. Sheep can be reintroduced into a former range but these populations sometimes fluctuate to qualitative and quantitative extremes. Bighorns have been reintroduced as stand-ins for the extinct Audubon's sheep in South Dakota's Badlands National Park and also in the Missouri River breaks in central Montana. These populations have done reasonably well and seem to be flourishing. In this process, relocating several animals from a given flock seems to be more effective than selecting individuals from several separate bands.

For those who might advocate a 'Yellowstone Park-hands off-Nature's way' approach to wildlife management, it may be appropriate to point out that populations of living things are profoundly affected by man and a variety of his activities. Countering those with calculated and positive forms of intervention is the only way to manage and help balance the scale. The human impact on the environment and wildlife is dramatic, long-lasting, and far-reaching. The current controversy surrounding the Yellowstone bison that wander out of the park during the winter snows, and then become a management problem for the state of Montana, is a case in point. These buffalo are being managed in Montana by a largely unpopular program of shooting them, and various interests including Native Americans, ranchers, environmentalists, preservationists, etc, are collectively displeased. Calves that follow the adults out of the park are unceremoniously slaughtered. Yellowstone is abdicating a responsibility that should more appropriately exist within the borders of the park. Yellowstone is a very valuable estate in terms of land, timber, wildlife, recreation and several other vital resources. To expect that nature or some other authority will oversee conditions there seems unwise.

Custer State Park, a popular but much smaller unit in South Dakota, could give lessons to the National Park Service in terms of recognizing the monetary and recreational value of what exists within its borders. The timber and wildlife therein, amongst which are buffalo, elk, and bighorns, subsist in accordance with the Park's 'carrying capacity'. In other words, the population numbers are limited in terms of what the environment there can support. Hunting and timber removal exists in a very carefully regulated way. Income is generated, resources are managed and overall this seems to be a very healthy system.

Nature's way may lead to an endangered status or even extinction, and some popular wildlife species worldwide are presently on that track. Natural populations in the purest sense may not presently exist, or at best they are very rare. When Nature's way was the norm there were no guarantees of species perpetuation. Extinction is a natural and non-preferential process. Wild sheep, along with other wildlife forms and their habitats, deserve our best efforts on their behalf, and in our own.

Perhaps this sounds like double-talk, but there are significant points in 'hands-on' or 'hands-off' approaches to wildlife management. The inter-relationships of living things are extremely complex and often inconspicuous, and in our management efforts we must not overlook the long term impact of our programs on all species and the physical environment. Management directed toward a single wildlife species is not plausible. The target organism is, after all, only one unit in an ecological system. A target organism apart from other species may not deserve or require favored treatment, at least not at the expense of other life forms or the entire system. The lion in sheep country, the wolf in Yellowstone, and the bear in the salmon stream are not enemies. Several years ago the comic strip character Pogo identified the enemy and declared it was us. Our baser qualities of ego, apathy, greed, indifference, pride and some other failings stand in the way of conservation and effective wildlife management practices.

Politics and economics present means for effective wildlife management, yet on the other hand these are the factors by which more of our wildlife may be lost. Our involvement is required, and participation in wildlife/conservation organizations and their efforts concentrate energy, understanding, and dollars, usually to the greater good. We must also consider the political scene and its relationship to these matters. Your opinion or individual vote may be insignificant, but when regional or national organizations vote their collective minds, a powerful presence is created.

Bighorns are born on the edge of the world. Left: Desert bighorn ewe. Above: Rocky Mountain bighorn. Below Left: Rocky Mountain bighorns. Below Right: Dall's ram. Opposite page (main pic): Bighorn lamb. Left: Badlands bighorns. Right: Desert bighorn ram.

Trophy ram

HUNTING

If there is controversy regarding the management of wildlife, the subject of hunting is even more likely to polarize opinions. The sequence of management and hunting is intentional, and hunting follows as an important management tool. It is a means of involvement that is not acceptable to some, and strongly supported by others.

During the mid- and late 1800s wild sheep and many other North American game animals were killed with impunity. Because of the enormous pressure upon these animals, game laws started to emerge state by state and species by species, beginning about 1895 in the United States. The importance of seasons, bag limits, and hunting ethics has become more evident and a number of game animals have regained footholds. Wild sheep populations in several areas are stable and healthy, while others struggle to survive. Regulated hunting offers an effective means to manage animal populations and gain the finances to accomplish the same. Managers are afforded biological data on particular species in particular habitats and the presence of parasites, disease, and details on population structure comes from data provided by hunters.

No other North American wildlife trophy animal is more highly regarded than a wild mountain ram. The insertion of a trophy animal into the Boone and Crockett (describing firearms and pickups) or the

. . . *the circle of life is small, but complete: The four rams who complete the circle – Above: Desert bighorn. Opposite page: Dall's. Below, far left: Rocky Mountain bighorn. Below left: Stone's.*

Pope and Young (archery) record book is a dream for many who hunt. To achieve this with a North American wild sheep is a particularly significant accomplishment. Occasionally luck plays a role but more often substantial investments of time and money are prerequisites. In 1994 a hunter bid and paid for a sheep permit in the state of Washington, and Washington received $90,000 from that sale to assist in wild sheep management programs.[12] The 1993 Governor's permit for a bighorn ram in Montana sold in auction for an amount in excess of $200,000. At least, some and perhaps all, of that amount went back into wildlife management in Montana. A Desert bighorn ram permit in southern Baja, California was purchased for $20,000 in the early 1990s. A 1997 report indicated that $400,000 was raised in auction by the sale of two special bighorn sheep tags in Alberta. The Rocky Mountain Elk Foundation and the Foundation for North American Wild Sheep were involved in these efforts.[13] Again money accrued to wild sheep and wildlife management, and there are many such stories and extremes.

In 1947 an article by Grantcel Fitz entitled 'Grand Slam of Sheep' appeared in *True* magazine.[14] In approximately 1956, the late Bob Housholder, loosely organized a club made up of a small number of individuals who had harvested at least one of all four varieties of North American wild sheep . . . a Grand Slam. This would make the Grand Slam Club one of the oldest organized hunting groups recognizing trophy animals and hunters. Housholder and Jack O'Connor were friends and enthusiastic about sheep hunting. Housholder developed a newsletter and devised a form that could be used to make application for membership to the group. The original group of only about half a dozen began to grow. O'Connor can be credited with popularization of the concept.

By the 1970s the fever of Grand Slam accomplishment had grabbed the attention of the hunting fraternity and during and prior to that time, the quest for a Desert bighorn to complete the series had resulted in numerous fiascos. The Desert bighorn was and is available in only very limited numbers. Several sheep hunters, all of whom should have known better, participated in illegal and unethical acquisition of trophy Desert rams. Sheep were poached, bought and sold, and state and national borders were violated by a number of hunters. Federal authorities became aware and involved, and there were many arrests and convictions, which included some prominent individuals.

The Grand Slam Club records were subpoenaed in this sting operation and the resulting posture in the club was cooperation and to disavow all memberships up to that point. Housholder, O'Connor and most of the membership were completely innocent and not involved in the illegalities in any way. The club started its membership all over again with an imperative of positive proof of the legalities for entry. As of April 1997 the membership of Grand Slam official and documented entries totals over 700.

There are archery successes by approximately eight individuals, and several legitimate and legal Grand Slam accomplishments in archery and firearms have not been entered, by the choice of the hunters. It is not required that these Grand Slam animals meet record book minimum standards to qualify, or that the hunters seek Grand Slam Club membership. Chuck Adams, a well known bowhunter, has the Grand Slam, and Tom Hoffman, a Pope and Young member from New York, has a double Grand Slam and these are popularly recognized. The club is presently operational in Birmingham, Alabama.

Jack O'Connor (1902-1978), who was known for his preference and enthusiasm for the .270 caliber Winchester rifle and cartridge, was one of the select charter group of Grand Slam firearms hunters. O'Connor, was an outstanding sportsman and the shooting editor for *Outdoor Life* magazine from 1941 to 1972. He served on the staff of *Hunting* magazine and was a prolific writer, scholar, teacher, and sheep hunter of considerable prowess. Jack O'Connor essentially 'wrote the book' for many enthusiasts to follow, and his magazine stories and books served to establish high ideals and ethical behaviors in the pursuit of game. Probably more than any other person, O'Connor raised the level of consciousness and interest in wild sheep, at least in hunting terms.

That some may bend the rules or ignore ethics in order to ingratiate themselves is not all that peculiar in any of several human enterprises. Sheep hunting is not immune and the temptations are great. There is a clear distinction between hunting which is descriptive of legal activity and poaching which relates to the alternate, just as there is in right and wrong. Record book entries also insist on a standard of 'fair chase' which imposes some other restrictions on the taking of game beyond simple legalities. Some of the details of 'fair chase' are presented as part of the Boone and Crockett figures (pages 48 and 49), which describes the scoring system for wild sheep.

A requisite in hunting sheep is physical conditioning, and few hunting experiences will be as demanding as that brought about by the mountainous terrain, the altitude, the temperatures, and other environmental extremes. A cardinal rule in sheep hunting is that you must see the sheep before the sheep see you.[15] Their phenomenal eyesight has been previously mentioned, so first class optics including a high quality spotting scope are important. Patient glassing and stealth in the approach are also part of the formula for success. The game is actually in the stalk, and the shot, assuming proper equipment and adequate practice, should be of less consequence. Rams are usually stationary and long shots or shots at running animals suggests failure in the stalk. In hunting sheep and many other species it is often productive to attain an elevation advantage. Sheep in particular expect danger from below, and as a consequence seldom watch for what is taking place above them.

A band of rams may seem to select locations where stalks are almost impossible, such as high 'saddles', with broad expanse basins below and on both sides. These wild sheep may choose a precipice with sides so steep and cover so sparse that concealment or approaches are not possible. The presence of one or more sentinels is also part of the line of defense against predation. These tactics might appear to be carefully reasoned and rational behaviors, but more

Above: Calm before the storm, Rocky Mountain bighorn rams. Opposite: Bighorn rams "pitch their best stuff" during the rut. Below: The "huddle" in peace . . . and war.

likely these group actions are conditioned by the negative experiences of survivors. Younger rams take their cues from the elders, so these effective tactics are learned and perpetuated. Sheep, deer, elk and no doubt many other game species learn what to do during hunting seasons. Their ranges and behaviors adjust to the season. Sanctuaries exist in formal and informal terms, and the skills of seasoned associates often removes the group from harm's way.

What constitutes a recognized trophy animal is established by strict guidelines which favor mass and symmetry. Points totals which are the equivalent of inches, position a specimen in the record book, or out of the record book, after specified drying periods. Overall length of the outside curve and circumferences at the quarters, tempered by asymmetrical deductions, constitute the essence of scoring sheep. The scoring/recording form used for North American wild sheep is provided as figures A and B to illustrate the system. The form is provided with permission of the Boone and Crockett Club in Missoula, Montana. The point requirements for a Pope and Young (archery) entry are 140 for either bighorn and 120 for either thinhorn. Boone and Crockett differentiates in terms of all-time book entries and their awards program. Their minimums of point totals are shown in figure A (page 48).

In more personal terms a hunter may select a trophy on the basis of personal preferences related to the physical makeup of the horns or on the basis of certain environmental or other circumstances, discounting the regimen of mass, symmetry, and the 'book'. Brooming or a lack thereof, curling below the

". . . before the sheep see you"

44

jaw, completion of the curl and passing above the bridge of the nose, the presence of lamb tips, close/tight curling, color, heavy bases, etc, all contribute to trophy assessment or beauty, which after all is in the eye of the beholder.

The degree of horn curl, like the number of points on a deer, is a relative factor and these conditions can mean very little in trophy terms. Unfortunately most state/province game departments continue to utilize the extent of the curl in terms of legalities. In their defense, curl is conspicuous; but the practice of brooming away the distal portion of the horn reduces the amount of curl. The tip segment that may come upward and pass the bridge of the nose can actually decrease a gross score. The presence of a lamb tip will move the circumference measurements away from the base and reduce their values. Circumference totals are taken at the quarters of the length of the outside curve; and a perfect long thin tapered horn displaces 2nd and 3rd quarter measurements into smaller areas of the horn.

In 1965, Nevada established an approach and an alternate definition of legality. Hunters were required to select a ram of at least 7 years of age or a Boone and Crockett score of at least 144 points. Spotting scopes of 15x and indoctrination were required. A few years later, the method was described as less than ideal. Combining or accepting alternates of curl and age ring minimums might be a format to consider.

Brooming is often an intentional act of close curled wild sheep that rub the ends of their horns on rough surfaces in order to shorten them and unblock vision.

The Sentinel

Blood brothers –
Rocky Mountain bighorn rams.

Lip curl or 'flehmen'

Tip portions may also be unintentionally lost in fighting. The thinhorn sheep may broom either intentionally or accidentally, but their horns usually flare and need not be broomed as frequently or severely.

Most wild rams are sexually active at 8 years of age, and when they are from 8 to 10 years of age they are most likely to be in a trophy class (full curls). A ram's sexual capability occurs much earlier and may even develop in the first year. However, the opportunities to exercise the capability are a function of the actions of adult rams and ewes. Generally age correlates with trophy quality and usually the older the better. This is not true with deer which must replace antler mass each year, and with extended age the antler formation falters. Ram specimens of 12-14 years are likely to be outstanding, and living beyond a dozen years is unusual.

Any wild North American ram with an outside curve of 40 inch (plus) horns, broomed or unbroomed is exceptional. Bases of 15-17 inches are of superior quality, and when the bulk of that mass carries forward through the curvature, the magical score of 200 points (inches) may be reached. Two hundred point rams are few and far between and only a select few in the record books are so large. Judging a trophy sheep on the basis of 1 or 2 inches, or sometimes only a fraction of a inch at 200-300 yards, is a practiced art, only attempted by an experienced few.

Rams tend to seek others of their general horn proportions and age groups, so when finding a lone large ram, it may be solitary, but more likely he will be part of a nearby group that share similar

Loner . . .

dimensions. Locating a bachelor group of large rams with choices and opportunity for comparison is the sheep hunter's goal. Other than during the rut, a mixed group of young, old, and medium sized males suggests that there may not be many rams in the region and perhaps a better area can be found.

A solitary ram is worth investigating. The older ones tire of the youthful ardor and because of tooth wear and resulting digestive upset, they become less sociable and tend to isolate themselves. It might also be that the loner has outlived his peer social group and he is the only one remaining. This would correlate with age and possible trophy status, and it may offer a more humane demise than might otherwise occur.

Regulated hunting provides the financial resources to assist in the management of game species and their allies. The 1937 Pittman-Robertson tax funds generated by sales of firearms, ammunition, and archery equipment has collectively produced almost $6,000,000,000 for use by government fish and wildlife agencies. Land purchases with Pittman-Robertson funds are used by the public and from 70 to 90% of these users are neither hunters or fishermen. In 1992 over $165,000,000 came from this 11% tax from willing sportsmen and sportswomen. More recent figures show $500,000,000 from the sale of about 15 million hunting licenses alone.[16] If hunting and fishing opportunities were curtailed by those who are opposed, how would the various programs which support game animals and all wildlife continue? The dollars invested each year by sheep hunters boggle the mind.

Broomed . . .

Desert bighorn ram

Figure A

Records of North American
Big Game

BOONE AND CROCKETT CLUB

Old Milwaukee Depot
250 Station Drive
Missoula, MT 59801

SHEEP   Kind of Sheep:_____

Minimum Score:	Awards	All-time
bighorn	175	180
desert	165	168
Dall's	160	170
Stone's	165	170

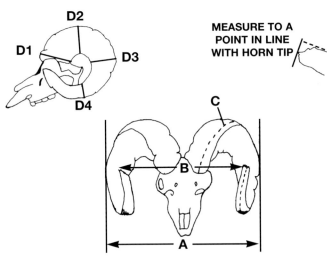

MEASURE TO A POINT IN LINE WITH HORN TIP

SEE OTHER SIDE FOR INSTRUCTIONS		Column 1	Column 2	Column 3
A. Greatest Spread (Is Often Tip to Tip Spread)		Right Horn	Left Horn	Difference
B. Tip to Tip Spread				
C. Length of Horn				
D-1. Circumference of Base				
D-2. Circumference at First Quarter				
D-3. Circumference at Second Quarter				
D-4. Circumference at Third Quarter				
TOTALS				
ADD	Column 1	Exact Locality Where Killed:		
	Column 2	Date Killed: By Whom Killed:		
SUBTOTAL		Present Owner:		
SUBTRACT Column 3		Owner's Address:		
FINAL SCORE		Guide's Name and Address:		
		Remarks: (Mention Any Abnormalities or Unique Qualities)		

I certify that I have measured this trophy on _____ 19 _____
at (address) _____ City _____ State _____
and that these measurements and data are, to the best of my knowledge and belief, made in accordance with the instructions given.

Witness: _____   Signature: _____

B&C OFFICIAL MEASURER [| |]
                              I.D. Number

Figure B

All measurements must be made with a 1/4-inch wide flexible steel tape to the nearest one-eighth of an inch. Wherever it is necessary to change direction of measurement, mark a control point and swing tape at this point. Enter fractional figures in eights, without reduction. Official measurements cannot be taken until horns have air dried for at least 60 days after the animal was killed.

A.   Greatest Spread is measured between perpendiculars at a right angle to the center line of the skull.

B.   Tip to Tip Spread is measured between tips of horns.

C.   Length of Horn is measured from the lowest point in front on outer curve to a point in line with tip. Do not press tape into depressions. The low point of the outer curve of the horn is considered to be the low point of the frontal portion of the horn, situated above and slightly medial to the eye socket (not the outside edge). Use a straight edge, perpendicular to horn axis, to end measurement on "broomed" horns.

D-1. Circumference of Base is measured at a right angle to axis of horn. Do not follow irregular edge of horn; the line of measurement must be entirely on horn material, not the jagged edge often noted.

D-2-3-4. Divide measurement C of longer horn by four. Starting at base, mark both horns at these quarters (even though the other horn is shorter) and measure circumferences at these marks, with measurements taken at right angles to horn axis.

FAIR CHASE STATEMENT FOR ALL HUNTER-TAKEN TROPHIES

FAIR CHASE, as defined by the Boone and Crockett Club, is the ethical, sportsmanlike and lawful pursuit and taking of any free-ranging wild game animal in a manner that does not give the hunter an improper or unfair advantage over such game animals.
Use of any of the following methods in the taking of game shall be deemed UNFAIR CHASE and unsportsmanlike:

I.   Spotting or herding game from the air, followed by landing in its vicinity for the purpose of pursuit and shooting;

I.   Spotting or herding game from the air, followed by landing in its vicinity for the purpose of pursuit and shooting;

II.   Herding, pursuing, or shooting game from any motorboat or motor vehicle;

III. Use of electronic devices for attracting, locating, or observing game, or for guiding the hunter to such game;

IV.   Hunting game confined by artificial barriers, including escape-proof fenced enclosures, or hunting game transplanted solely for the purpose of commercial shooting;

V.   Taking of game in a manner not in full compliance with the game laws or regulations of the federal government or of any state, province, territory, or tribal council on reservations or tribal lands;

VI.   Or as may otherwise be deemed unfair or unsportsmanlike by the Executive Committee of the Boone and Crockett Club.

I certify that the trophy scored on this chart was taken in FAIR CHASE as defined above by the Boone and Crockett Club. In signing this statement, I understand that if this entry is found to be fraudulent, it will not be accepted into the Awards program and all of my prior entries are subject to deletion from future editions of Records of North American Big Game and future entries may not be accepted.

Date: _____ Signature of Hunter: _____
                                        (Have signature notarized by a Notary Public.)

Rocky Mountain bighorn ram

TAXONOMY

The science of taxonomy and the system of sorting living things is not so precise as intended because biological and evolutionary relationships are not always completely clear, or without some controversy. There are many paleontological 'pages' missing and there are occasional divergent expert views, terms, and applications. Taxonomy lacks mathematical precision, yet it has permitted organization of life forms into manageable and recognizable groups. It has clearly defined most relationships and physiological trends, bringing order and systematics into creation's life forms. This system also permits ease of deletion (extinction) and addition (discovery) of new forms.

Aristotle attempted a systematic inventory but Karl Von Linne (*Linnaeus*—Latinized) is credited with the current system, which introduced order in 1753 as the *Systema Naturae*. The original work related to plants and the genius of *Linnaeus* was his creation of a binomial (two name) system. This utilized two names, a genus and a species for all living things. Common names had, and still have no order, no continuity, and no limit. A species or a kind of living thing is more accurately constituted as the members of a breeding kind. The two names of genus and species are arranged with the genus, a noun being first. The genus is somewhat like a family surname. The species, the second name, is typically an adjective and it actually describes the kind, with a Latin term. Using the species in combination with the genus represents the starting place, or the bottom line, in a sequence of classification. The species, or second name is also called the trivial name. No plant or animal can have the same binomial name, but like John, Jose, or Emily . . . familiaris, domestica, alba and several other species names are used frequently. Our sequence begins with a plant or animal species, like *Ovis canadensis* Shaw, the bighorn, crediting the original scientific investigator who studied and named the life form.

Taxonomy proceeds in a hierarchy from the species (genus and species) through several successive levels of complexity, organization, and relationships concluding with the largest subgroup of living things, the Kingdom. The Kingdoms may be from two (Plant and Animal) to five in number. Bacteria, Blue-green algae, Algae, Fungi, Higher Plants, Protozoa, and Animals are arranged according to authority. So in a hierarchy order or a descending progression, the sequence is Kingdom, Phylum, Class, Order, Family, Genus and Species; like the series: book, chapter, and verse. Super- and Sub- are prefix terms applied above and below the standard levels in order to create special levels. Other special groups are tribes and varieties or races (subspecies), both of which apply to our interest group, *Ovis*. The special groups are important to further define life forms.

The relationships are presented and defined in terms of an evolutionary context, under the descriptive term phylogeny. 'Phylogeny' describes the overall development of the biological group, as opposed to the development of the individual, which is termed

Ovis canadensis nelsoni (borrego, cimmaron) Nelson

ontogeny. The development of the individual often 'mirrors' the development of the biological group. Phylogeny reflects anatomy, physiology, biochemistry, embryology, genetics, paleontology, geography, ethology (behavior), and some of science's best efforts. So now in the Latinized and systematized form our North American wild sheep are described as follows:

Kingdom: Animalia. Multicellular organisms that require plant or animal substance as food.

Phylum: Chordata. Animals with a notochord, a dorsal hollow nerve cord, and pharyngeal gill slits at some time. This describes the higher life forms and some obscure aquatic forms.

Subphylum: Vertebrata. Spinal cord is enclosed by a bony vertebral column, a segmented body and a brain protected by a skull (approximately 43,000 species of fish, amphibians, reptiles, birds, and mammals).

Class: Mammalia. Young nourished by milk glands; breathing by lungs, a diaphragm divides the body cavity. Skin with hair, constant warm body temperature, red blood cells without nuclei (approximately 5,000 living species).

Order: Ungulata. Hoofed herbivores. Includes the even-toed, and the odd-toed horses, tapirs, and rhinos, etc.

SubOrder: Artiodactyla. Even-toed (cloven hoof) ungulates. Also camels, hippos, and many domestic species; about 200 species.

Family: Bovidae. Ruminants with hollow and unbranched horns. Oxen, sheep, goats. Also includes bison, musk ox, and bighorns.

Tribe: Caprinae. Sheep, goats, and the Saiga.

Genus: Ovis. Sheep, including living and extinct,

Ovis canadensis canadensis Shaw

new and old-world forms such as the Aoudad, Mouflon, Bharal, Urial, Tur, Argali, Marco Polo sheep, the domestics, and North American wild sheep — *Ovis sp.*

Species (binomial): *Ovis canadensis* Shaw Bighorns *Ovis dalli* Nelson Thinhorns.

Subspecies: Bighorns:

Ovis canadensis canadensis Shaw, with a wide range in Canada and the USA . . . the Rocky Mountain bighorn.

Ovis canadensis californiana Douglas; California bighorn, existing irregularly east of the Cascades and into southern British Columbia.

Reflecting upon . . .

Ovis canadensis auduboni Merriam; Audubon's or Badlands bighorn, (extinct).

Ovis canadensis nelsoni (borrego, cimmaron) Nelson; Desert bighorn sheep.

Ovis canadensis mexicana Merriam; Mexican bighorn.

Ovis canadensis cremnobates Elliot; Peninsular bighorn.

Ovis canadensis weemsi Goldman; Baja bighorn.

Thinhorns:

Ovis dalli dalli Nelson; Dall's Sheep, Dall Sheep, White Sheep.

O.dalli kenaiensis Allen; a recognized Alaskan Kenai Peninsula subspecies.

Ovis dalli stonei Allen; Stone's Sheep, Stone Sheep, Black sheep with regional varieties includes Fannin's Sheep, an intermediate form recognized by some.

'Mountain Sheep' is a designation applied to both species of North American wild sheep, Bighorn, and Thinhorn and it also includes a Siberian 'cousin', the snow sheep, *Ovis (Pachyceros) nivicola*. *Pachyceros* means 'thick horn' and these three species can be collected under a Subgenus-Pachyceros, which excludes the other old-world forms (essentially the Argalis, the Mouflons, the Urials, and others).

This organizational scheme can be applied to all living things and although the system may appear to be burdensome (particularly to the freshman biology student), it establishes a systematic, organized approach to animal and plant classification and evolutionary prehistory. So for those who like or appreciate organization, it is a beautiful system and for those who do not, it persists as a complex mystery of science.

BIGHORNS & THINHORNS

In an extension of the topic, biologists-taxonomists are in two camps, the 'lumpers' and the 'splitters'. One gathers the varieties of a particular life form into as few units as possible and the other differentiates in as many ways as possible creating a greater number of units. So in the extremes of lumping and splitting, the North American wild sheep might conceivably be a single species, while there are arguments for four, five, six, or seven species. The consensus is that there are two, and in common language we are settling on bighorns and thinhorns. The differences in habitat and physical characteristics have yielded four major type variations: the Desert bighorn, the Rocky Mountain bighorn, Dall's sheep and Stone's sheep. There are many (15-20) subspecies and variations or 'races' of wild sheep, but most of these show little distinction from each other. Most authorities will agree on 10 subspecies. The 'saddleback sheep' or Fannin's sheep is thought to be an intermediate form between Dall's sheep and Stone's sheep. There are color variations, size variations, and geographical variations or distinctions, but most of the 'races' are only slightly different or are intergradations which are less than precise and not an important part of this effort. Races are geographically distinct or isolated and feature some differences in physical characteristics. Species and their separations are reflective of reproductive isolation, which is not always an adequate or an accurate basis.

. . . youth and maturity

57

DESERT BIGHORNS

Desert sheep are somewhat smaller than the Rocky Mountain bighorns, with rams standing about 35 inches at the shoulder and weighing from 150 to 180 pounds. They tend to be lean and angular, unlike the more blocky Rocky Mountain or California bighorns. Their coats are also better adapted to the hot dry conditions, not only in terms of thickness but also in coloration.

Moisture is a severe limiting factor in the habitat of the Desert sheep. Much of their requirement for water is taken from the xerophytic desert plants that typically retain water. The barrel cactus is a favored source, and cacti are used extensively. Available water in tanks or ponds concentrates these sheep at specific times in specific locations, and competition for this resource; intra- and interspecies, is extreme.

The breeding season is other than what was described previously for wild sheep overall. These ewes are bred between July and October and the young are born over a longer period, not limited by snow, ice, or available forage. The Desert sheep diets are also dissimilar. These wild sheep are unable to exist by grazing on the scarce desert grasses and other soft plant material. Desert sheep browse opportunistically on a large variety of desert flora.

Desert sheep exist in Utah, New Mexico, Nevada, Arizona, west Texas, California, Colorado and into Mexico. One variety of Desert bighorn, the Peninsular bighorn sheep of southeastern California and the Baja, is suffering in extreme terms from a combination of factors that impact most and perhaps all of the North American wild sheep. A combination of negative conditions can be devastating. Contact with domestic and feral animals, impact of human activity, predation, disease and parasitic problems related to stress and environmental difficulty are involved. Water in this setting is never abundant, but quantities have been diminished by an introduction of the Tamarisk, or Salt Cedar plant. These plants require tremendous volumes of water which tends to reduce the limited quantities available for sheep and other wildlife. In some portions of this range, as many as 90% of the lambs have been lost. Lion kills of the lambs and some adults are evident. Respiratory pneumonia from bacteria and viruses acquired from domestic sheep and cattle is contributing to the deaths, and probably to the predation as well. The vitality of this relatively small population is particularly vulnerable.[17] Climate and nutrition are both contributive to successful reproduction.

Wild Desert sheep are of relatively small and widely distributed populations and they are difficult to locate by biologists and hunters, so supply and demand conditions are extreme and opportunities to study or hunt are rare and expensive.

The barrier to completing a Grand Slam usually exists with Desert sheep. Poaching and other unscrupulous behaviors relating to possession of a Desert ram are unfortunately too common. This was a substantially greater problem 20 years ago. The amounts paid to legally harvest one of these rams are very high, and a person who is willing and able to afford these fees may also conceivably be able to entice others in helping him break the law and engage in unethical practices. This is not to assert anything other than a means and a motivation for an illegal harvest. Certainly most wild sheep, including the Desert sheep, are tagged by responsible and ethical hunters in full compliance with the law of the state or province and with fair chase practices. Current scrutiny includes a step in the process called 'plugging'. A legally harvested animal in the 'lower 48' is categorically established and certified by the insertion of a quantified and/or qualified non-removable metallic plug into the base of the horn. This attests to the ownership and the legitimacy of possession. Sheep horns without the plug raises the 'red flag'. The plugging process is controlled by state or province authority.

The Desert Bighorn Council was formed in 1957 to consider factors related to the well-being of this species. The Council is made up of professional and amateur members, concerning themselves with the survival of the Desert bighorn. It is certainly the most vulnerable of all of the North American wild sheep, and it may also be the best representative of valued wild animals and the problems that wildlife experience. Man's activities, ranging from the Spanish explorations in the 1500s through the creation of ski lifts and tramways in modern times, have imposed upon Desert bighorns. Poaching, ranching, mineral exploration, fences, highways, pollution and other human intrusions have impacted these wild sheep, and perhaps have moved them collectively to the brink.

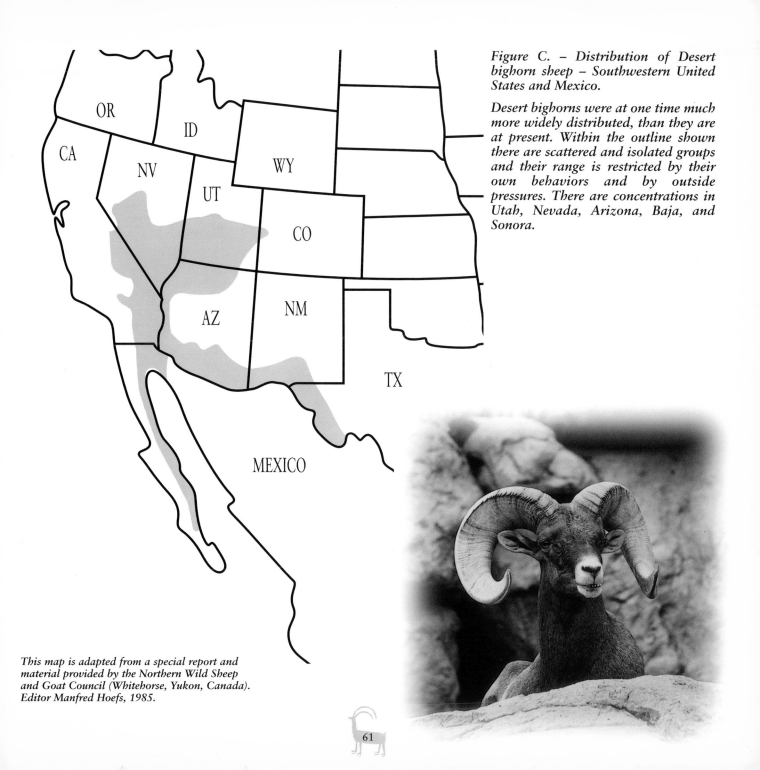

Figure C. – Distribution of Desert bighorn sheep – Southwestern United States and Mexico.

Desert bighorns were at one time much more widely distributed, than they are at present. Within the outline shown there are scattered and isolated groups and their range is restricted by their own behaviors and by outside pressures. There are concentrations in Utah, Nevada, Arizona, Baja, and Sonora.

OR

ID

CA

NV

WY

UT

CO

AZ

NM

TX

MEXICO

This map is adapted from a special report and material provided by the Northern Wild Sheep and Goat Council (Whitehorse, Yukon, Canada). Editor Manfred Hoefs, 1985.

61

G. Tillett
© 1996

ROCKY MOUNTAIN BIGHORNS

It is this particular wild sheep that is most familiar and most wide-spread throughout the western portions of the United States and Canada. The map provided (figure D) helps to describe distribution. These bighorns are also larger in body than the other North American wild sheep, and the premier specimens, in terms of body size and horn mass, reside in Montana, and in Alberta, Canada. Wyoming may have the largest population in the United States. A large male may extend 5 feet in length and be 40 inches at the shoulder. Girth at the chest may on occasion exceed 48 inches, and the mass of the head, neck and shoulders are striking features. They may reach 300 pounds or more in the case of mature rams.

The coat color of the Rocky Mountain bighorns varies with the individual and with the season. Many have a rich chocolate coat and pelage becomes less attractive during shedding in the transition to warmer months. The hair may also appear gray-brown, with a sometimes purplish cast. The hair closely resembles that of elk, at least in texture and in terms of the soft under fur which protects against the cold. The horns of the Rocky Mountain bighorn rams tend toward tighter curls, and as a consequence brooming is very common. The portions of the distal horn that restrict vision and encourage the act are sometimes inserted in rock crevices and broken off in that way.

It is believed that the ancestors of today's North American wild sheep populations are directly related to the Rocky Mountain bighorn, and that it was those that made the successful trek across the Bering Strait, during the Pleistocene period. Glacial ice at some point separated northern and southern groups, contributing to the creation of our two species.

Rocky Mountain bighorns are serving as 'stand-ins' to replace the extinct Audubon's and Badlands bighorns eliminated from their range in the Dakotas and nearby states. In 1964, in Badlands National Park, Southwestern South Dakota, 22 bighorns (16 ewes and 6 rams) were introduced from Pike's Peak in Colorado. They were kept in a 370-acre enclosure in the park with the idea of transplanting from there into the Black Hills and into the Badlands. When in 1967 it appeared the wild sheep were not doing well in the enclosure, and the population diminished to about 14 remaining, the gates were opened and the sheep were released. Ted Benzon, a biologist with the South Dakota Department of Game, Fish and Parks estimates that today the herd numbers about 150 and that this small group may be 'the best quality herd of Rocky Mountain bighorns in the lower 48'. Benzon advises that there are a number of 'class four' (full curl) rams in the population. He explains that the big rams have considerable mass and width and are 'fantastic'. In a sting operation, a wildlife official offered $20,000 for a poached ram skull from the Badlands. The individual held out for $40,000, but received legal sanctions and no money.

There seems to be no serious health problem in this group, but in one instance in 1992 lungworm was found in a dead lamb. Studies indicate that other areas of the park are adequate to support sheep in terms of their needs for forage, water, escape terrain, and lambing. There may be a potential for as many as 800 wild sheep in these badlands. About 16 animals have been recently relocated within the boundaries and they appear to be doing well.

'Bighorns' won a recent victory in Federal District Court (Oregon), which related to a conflict of interest with the (domestic) sheep industry and Rocky Mountain bighorns in a portion of Hell's Canyon and the Snake River between Oregon and Idaho. Speculation is that the area can support several thousand wild sheep. Approximately 200 of the Bighorns were transplanted there in the 1970s and thereafter, but 20 years later the wild sheep population was only between 20 and 30 animals. There were documented reports of the Bighorns dying in just a short time after nose-to-nose contact with domestic sheep. On occasion, the wild sheep were shot in order to prevent their contact with others of their kind. The United States Forest Service, the National Wildlife Federation, and other related interest groups pressed the issue and the Court determined that 'if there is a conflict between bighorn and domestic sheep, the bighorn have priority'.

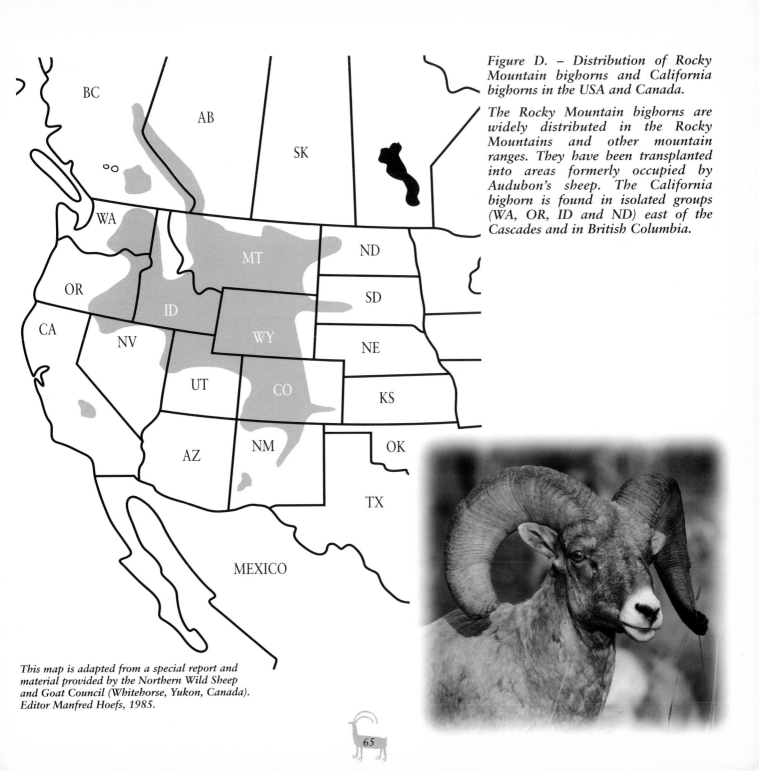

Figure D. – Distribution of Rocky Mountain bighorns and California bighorns in the USA and Canada.

The Rocky Mountain bighorns are widely distributed in the Rocky Mountains and other mountain ranges. They have been transplanted into areas formerly occupied by Audubon's sheep. The California bighorn is found in isolated groups (WA, OR, ID and ND) east of the Cascades and in British Columbia.

BC

AB

SK

WA

OR

CA

NV

ID

MT

WY

UT

AZ

NM

CO

ND

SD

NE

KS

OK

TX

MEXICO

This map is adapted from a special report and material provided by the Northern Wild Sheep and Goat Council (Whitehorse, Yukon, Canada). Editor Manfred Hoefs, 1985.

65

G. TILLETT
©1997

DALL'S SHEEP

Dall's sheep (or Dall sheep or white sheep) were named for W. H. Dall, an Alaskan explorer. This is probably the most beautiful of all wild sheep, and it is regarded by many as the most beautiful of all wild game animals. The coat is pure white, the eyes are a striking yellow, and the pale horns flare away from the head in symmetrical flowing curves. These sheep exist in the most spectacular of habitats in Alaska, including Kenai, the Yukon, the Northwest Territories, and the northwest corner of British Columbia. British Columbia recognizes four races of mountain sheep; Dall's, Stone's, Rocky Mountain bighorn, and California bighorn.[18] The distribution of white sheep is extensive, and the population is large and stable, at least in comparative terms.

Dall's sheep are generally accessible to hunters, photographers, and others with interest. There are sizable populations in the state and national parks of Alaska, giving many people the opportunity to see and appreciate them. Denali National Park, and Mount McKinley in the Alaskan Range, is one such place. The Chugach Mountains, Wrangell National Park, and the Wrangell Mountains are also good locations for Dall's sheep. The north slope of the Brooks Range near the Arctic National Wildlife Refuge also supports large numbers of these mountain sheep.

The Dall's, *O. dalli,* are found over a large north to south range and the color phase darkens as one moves

67

toward the south. Black hair becomes evident, the tail goes from white to black, and a dark 'saddle' is evident on some. The subspecies are color and size intergradations into the Fannin's, or saddleback sheep, and to the Stone's sheep or black (salt and pepper) sheep. Stone's sheep coloration is a little like the ptarmigan between seasonal extremes. Within some groups in the middle range both very dark and very light sheep are evident.

Those who wish to hunt sheep would discover a number of opportunities available for Dall's rams, and they would find current costs from $6,000 to $10,000 in terms of outfitter charges alone. One must also consider transportation, equipment, licensing, and sometimes trophy fees or taxidermy. These trophy hunts usually extend from 7 to 12 days, in part to accommodate extremes in weather.

The horn structure of the Dall's rams and other thinhorns tend to include heavy bases and many are 12 to 14 inches, and perhaps 15 inches before drying. Dall's ram horns are often triangular in cross section, while those of the Stone's and the bighorns are generally oval. A prominent ridge follows the curvature along the outside edge of the Dall's, and the cleaned horns are pale yellow. Stone's ram horns are light or medium brown and the bighorns tend toward grey or darker brown. The trophy white sheep range around and above 36 inches of curvature and 40 inch specimens are much more common than they are with bighorns. Lamb tips are often present and curls can exceed 'full', or above the bridge of the nose. The mass is substantially less than that of the southern forms.

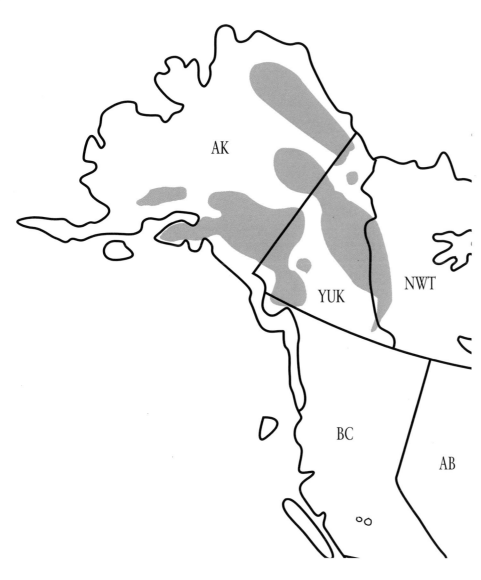

Figure E. – Distribution of Dall's sheep in the USA and Canada.

Dall's sheep are wide spread in the mountain ranges of Alaska, Yukon, Northwest Territories and into British Columbia. In Alaska populations exist in the Brooks Range, Tanana/Yukon Uplands, Alaskan Ranges East and West, the Talkeetna Mountains, The Wrangells, The Chugach and Kenai Mountains. In the Northwest Territories these sheep are primarily in the Mackenzie Mountains. The Yukon sheep are found in the British, the Ogilvie, and the St. Elias Mountains.

This map is adapted from a special report and material provided by the Northern Wild Sheep and Goat Council (Whitehorse, Yukon, Canada). Editor Manfred Hoefs, 1985.

G. TILLETT
©1997

STONE'S SHEEP

Stone's (Stone or black) sheep occupy ranges that are much less accessible than those of their northern white cousins. They are indigenous to the northern portions of British Columbia and the lower Yukon. These animals were named for Andrew Stone in approximately 1897. Stone was from Missoula, Montana and he was the first to collect, with scientific intentions, specimens of this sheep. Stone's sheep extend south toward the Peace and Skeena Rivers. The northern habitat limits of the Rocky Mountain bighorns extend almost to this habitat boundary, but the two occupancies do not overlap. An overlap to the north is common with Dall's sheep, and it can be difficult to differentiate Stone's and Dall's. Expeditions in the Cassiar region of British Columbia and to the Pelly Mountains of the Yukon are likely to produce Stone's sheep. For hunters, outfitting costs tend to be greater and the time required to locate these sheep is also increased to about two weeks. Costs run from about $9,000 to $13,000. Trophy fees are common and the season begins in August. The success rate on hunting Stone's rams is generally high and the darker forms are usually preferred.

Stone's sheep are mostly larger than Dall's and the color variations are from almost black, to white, with the darker forms inhabiting the southern portion of the range. The lighter ones intergrade with the white sheep in the north, and intermediate forms (Fannin's sheep) are likewise intermediate in distribution. Fannin's sheep, when and where recognized, are grouped with Stone's sheep. A mature Stone's ram may weigh over 200 pounds and stand 38-40 inches at the shoulder. Stone's sheep horns are more like those of the Dall's ram – wide spread or flaring. Stone's will sometimes exhibit an 'Argali' configuration, which remains tight against the skull to the jaw before the ends flare outward. This conformation is attractive and it generally describes the configuration of the Chadwick ram, the finest North American trophy ram ever taken by a hunter.

The Chadwick ram story was presented in *Outdoor Life* magazine in February 1937. L. S. Chadwick was essentially looking for 'camp meat' during a sheep hunt in a section of the Rocky Mountains, north of the Peace River in British Columbia. Chadwick and three other hunters, along with their guides Hargreaves, Golata, and Cochrane, were hunting the Muskwa River area. Rough and remote, the region had been exposed to the lightest of hunting pressure, so the hunters had trophy aspirations.

It was August 27, 1936, around mid afternoon, when that part of the group which included Chadwick, found three rams on a skyline during their spotting scope activities. The distance was too great for an immediate stalk, so pursuit was delayed until the next morning. Setting out on horseback, the small party arrived in the vicinity at lunch time. The rams were spotted at a distance of more than a mile and at least one of these sheep seemed to be in the trophy category.

The distance was closed to a couple of hundred yards, and Chadwick elected to use film instead of firearms. A decision was then made to try a shot at the largest ram, which was considerably below the hunter's position. The huge ram was hit low in the body, and as the band sprinted quickly down the slope and was starting up the other side, Chadwick fired additional shots. Chadwick and Hargreaves were immediately in pursuit and Hargreaves, who was in a better position and who was more agile than his companion, finished the action. The ram fell dead into a deep ravine. Initially there was some disappointment with the hunters because the body was so small . . . at least for the size of the horns. The tape revealed 52⅛ inches on the left horn, 31¼ inches between tips, and bases over 15 inches. The right horn had a missing tip of an estimated two inches. Chadwick was aware that the largest Stone's sheep on record was under 50 inches, so this would obviously establish a new world record. Frank Golata who held the horses during the drama, joined the group and the meat, cape, and horns were loaded after only a short carry.

This fine specimen, the property of the National Collection of Heads and Horns, can be viewed in the Buffalo Bill Historic Center, Cody, Wyoming. In addition to Chadwick's ram, William F. Cody's museum offers insight into a number of western, historic, and wildlife perspectives. It would also be worthwhile to visit the offices of the Foundation for North American Wild Sheep – FNAWS, which is nearby. Their current theme of 'putting sheep on the mountain' demonstrates inspiration and commitment of resources, in keeping the ones that are presently there, and restoring them to where they once were.

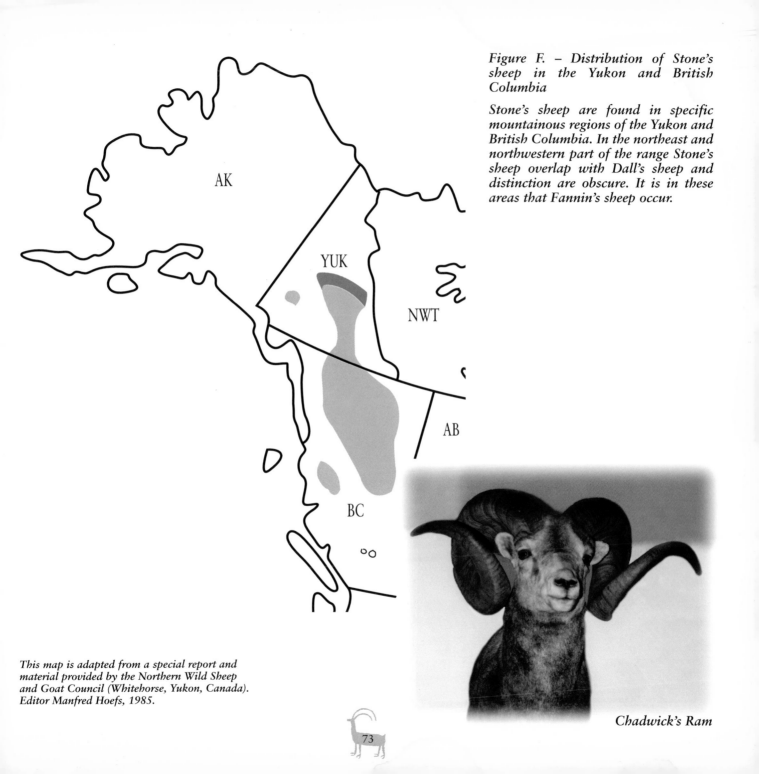

Figure F. – Distribution of Stone's sheep in the Yukon and British Columbia

Stone's sheep are found in specific mountainous regions of the Yukon and British Columbia. In the northeast and northwestern part of the range Stone's sheep overlap with Dall's sheep and distinction are obscure. It is in these areas that Fannin's sheep occur.

AK

YUK

NWT

AB

BC

This map is adapted from a special report and material provided by the Northern Wild Sheep and Goat Council (Whitehorse, Yukon, Canada). Editor Manfred Hoefs, 1985.

73

Chadwick's Ram

ENDNOTES

1   *Bering Strait*, Jack O'Connor, *The Art of Hunting Big Game in North America*, Book Division, Times Mirror Magazines Inc. (1977), p. 140.
2   *Body Language*, Valerius Geist and Michael Francis, *Wild Sheep Country*, Northword Press (1993), multiple entries.
3   *Sheep/Goat Shelter* Ernest Thompson Seton, *Lives of Game Animals*, Volume Three, Part II, Hoofed Animals, Doubleday, Doran, and Company Inc. (1929), p. 556.
4   *Sheep Disease*, Mark G. Sullivan, 'Return of the Bighorns,' *Montana Outdoors*, (November/ December 1996), p. 6.
5   *Three Mountain Sheep*, Mauricio Mixco, 'Kiliwa Mountain Sheep Traditions' in Gary Paul Nabhan (ed) *Counting Sheep*, University of Arizona Press (1993), pp. 38-40.
6   *Sheep Horn Trees*, Seton, p. 529.
7   *Sheep Carcasses*, Anita Alvarez DeWilliams, 'Bighorn Ethnohistory in Baja California' in Nabhan, pp. 51-52.
8   *Sheep Traps*, George Frison, *Prehistoric Hunters of the High Plains*, Academic Press, New York (1978), pp. 257-270.
9   *Horn Bows*, Reginald and Gladys Laubin, *American Indian Archery*, University of Oklahoma Press (1980), pp. 73-103.
10 *Sheepeaters*, Robert F. and Yolanda Murphy, *Handbook of North American Indians*, Volume 11 Great Basin, Smithsonian Institution (1986), pp. 288-89.
11 *Audubon Sheep*, Sullivan, p. 4.
12 *Washington Management*, Tom Pawlacyk, 'A Record Book Ram,' *Wild Sheep*, Foundation for North American Wild Sheep (Winter 1994-95), p. 65.
13 *Alberta: RMEF and FNAWS*, 'Forum,' *Wild Sheep*, Foundation for North American Wild Sheep (Winter 1996-97), p. 17.
14 *Grand Slam*, O'Connor, p. 342.
15 *Hunting Rule*, O'Connor, p. 137.
16 *Hunting Licenses*, Leland Speakes Jr, 'First Vice President's Message,' *Wild Sheep*, Foundation for North American Wild Sheep (Fall 1996), p. 4.
17 *Peninsular Bighorn*, Bob Holmes, 'Up Against Steep Odds,' *National Wildlife*, National Wildlife Federation (February/March 1997), pp. 46-55.
18 *British Columbia Sheep*, Byron W. Dalrymple, *North American Game Hunter*, Stoeger Publishing Company (1974), p. 276.

BIBLIOGRAPHY

Carkhuff, James L. 'Great Arc of the Wild Sheep Guides,' Wild Sheep, Foundation for North American Wild Sheep, Winter 1996-97.
Dalrymple, Byron W. North American Game Hunting, Stoeger Publishing Company 1974.
Editor. 'Forum,' Wild Sheep, Foundation for North American Wild Sheep, Winter 1996-1997.
Frison, George. Prehistoric Hunters of the High Plains, Academic Press Inc., 1978.
Geist, Valerius. 'On the Management of Mountain Sheep,' North American Big Game-North American Big Game Awards, Seventh Edition, Boone and Crockett and the National Rifle Association, 1977.
Geist, Valerius and Michael Francis. Wild Sheep Country, Northword Press 1993.
Higginbotham, Billy and Don W. Steinbach. 'Things May Get Worse Before They Get Worser,' Wild Sheep, Foundation for North American Wild Sheep, Fall 1996.
Holmes, Bob. 'Up Against Steep Odds,' National Wildlife, National Wildlife Federation, February/March 1997.
Nabhan, Gary Paul. Counting Sheep, University of Arizona Press, 1993.
Laubin, Reginald and Gladys. American Indian Archery, University of Oklahoma Press, 1980.
Murphy, Robert F. and Yolanda. Handbook of North American Indians, Volume 11 Great Basin, Smithsonian Institution, 1986.
Monson, Gale and Lowell Sumner, The Desert Bighorn, The Univeristy of Arizona Press, 1990.
O'Connor, Jack. The Art of Big Game Hunting in North America, Book Division, Times Mirror Magazines, 1977.
Pawlacyk, Tom. 'A Record Book Ram,' Wild Sheep, Federation of North American Wild Sheep. Winter 1994-1995.
Schaafsma, Polly. The Rock Art of Utah, University of Utah Press, 1994.
Seton, Ernest Thompson. Lives of Game Animals, Volume Three, Part II, Hoofed Animals, Doubleday, Doran, and Company Inc. 1929.
Speakes, Leland Jr. 'First Vice President's Message,' Wild Sheep, Fall 1996.
Sullivan, Mark G. 'Return of the Bighorns,' Montana Outdoors, November/December 1996.